RESTORED FOR WAR

From Victim to Victor: The Metamorphosis of a Chosen Daughter

WRITTEN AND PUBLISHED BY:

Samantha Schaaf

For though we walk in the flesh we do not **war** in the flesh.

2 Corinthians 10:3 NKJV

Fight the good **fight** of faith, lay hold on eternal life, to which you were also called and have confessed the good confession in the presence of many witnesses.   1 Timothy 6:12 NKJV

Put on the whole **armor** of God, that you may be able to stand against the wiles of the devil.   Ephesians 6:11 NKJV

"...**Occupy** till I come."   Luke 19:13 NKJV

And from the days of John the Baptist until now the kingdom of heaven suffers **violence**, and the **violent** take it by **force**.

Matthew 11:12 NKJV

You therefore must endure hardship as a good **soldier** of Jesus Christ. No one engaged in **warfare** entangles himself with the affairs of *this* life, that he may please him who **enlisted** him as a **soldier**.   2Timothy 2:3-4 NKJV

ISBN: 979-8-218-50097-9

Editors: Olivia Schaaf and Raeann Rorie

For information email: contact@bondagebreakerbrigade.com

Table of Contents:

Introduction

This is the story of my life – the testimony of death to life, suffering to joy.

I owe Jesus **everything**.

As I take you through my life, I will explain things as they happened. Please understand that for any incident or person I talk about, the Lord has helped me to completely forgive them and replace what once was hatred with an indescribable love. It is my desire to see anyone that has ever caused me harm to be saved. That in and of itself is a miracle; only Jesus can take a broken heart and soul and put it back together again, causing the victim to forgive the offender and ask the Lord to save them, too. He helped me forgive myself too, which, to be honest, was probably the hardest considering all of the terrible things I have done. But even my own sins, no matter how extreme, were not more powerful than the Blood of Jesus. For that, I am forever thankful.

My prayer is that every single person reading this will receive breakthrough and freedom and that the devil's lies will be exposed. If God can take someone like me and totally heal and deliver them, nothing is impossible for anyone else.

Who I was before Christ was nothing short of broken, hateful, and unloving. He took a broken, forgotten, fearful, dead, neglected young woman and transformed her into a bold, chosen daughter.

Just like Jesus did, I am choosing to make myself of no reputation, sharing the deepest, darkest parts of my life so that Jesus may be lifted up to all men.

For I am not ashamed of the gospel of Christ, for it is the power of God to salvation for everyone who believes, for the Jew first and also for the Greek. Romans 1:16 NKJV

And they overcame him by the Blood of the Lamb and by the word of their testimony, and they did not love their lives to the death. Revelation 12:11 NKJV

Chapter 1

Rejected Before Day One

Many people experience satan trying to take them out of this world from a very young age. I was one of them. In fact, he tried to take me out before I ever breathed my first breath. I have been told two different stories of when my mother was pregnant with me, so it may be one or both that occurred, but only God knows the whole truth. One story is that my father very heavily tried to convince my mother to abort me, and another is that I was almost aborted due to a doctor's error. I was told that when my mother was about four months pregnant with me, she went to a doctor's appointment in which they did an ultrasound. They told my mother there was no heartbeat. The nurse even had the doctor double-check. They sent her home and said to her that if her body didn't naturally expel my remains, she would need to come in the following week for a D&C. When she went back in, the doctors thankfully checked one last time for my heartbeat, and there it was! This was one of the many times the Lord would save me from the hands of the enemy.

I am the second born of my mother and the first of my father. My parents were not married and had a very rocky relationship, to say the least. There were many physical and verbal altercations. Though I can't remember because of how young I was, I was told many stories and shown police reports of my father going after my mother with a gun and trying to shoot her, once even outside of a police station. Alongside that, my mother was a practicing "white witch" (there is no such thing; all witchcraft is evil). She apparently commonly did spells and played with Ouija boards when I was a baby. I didn't find out until many years later when receiving deliverance, that she had done spells on me. Demons of witchcraft confirmed that they came in through that open door when I was just a child, and they wouldn't leave until I renounced those spells on her behalf and forgave her. When sharing my testimony with my dad about the deliverance I received, he told me all kinds of stories of the spells and things that my mother would do and how she carried around a Bible while doing so.

I have also been told many different stories of my baby and toddler years. My dad claims that my mother abandoned me for a period of 2-3 years, leaving me in the care of my dad and grandparents on his side. This seems to be credible information as my mother has no baby pictures of me. I remember living with my mother around the age of 5 when I began kindergarten. Those years began some of the worst times of my life.

My mother had married my two younger sisters' dad around this time. My younger sisters' dad sexually, physically, and verbally abused me for many years. Because I was so young, I cannot say when the first incident occurred, but I can say it happened from at least 4 or 5 until I was 10 or 11 years old. My very first memory of the abuse is in the apartment we stayed in in Saint Charles. I lived there with my mom, older sister, and stepdad. My stepdad was very strict, and I was often in trouble for the most minor things. This would result in him sending me to my room for hours on end, in which he would come into the room and sexually or physically abuse me, sometimes both.

Around this time, every instance I was sent to my room, he would require me to be naked, and he would later come into my room and pin me down and molest me. I also recall him coming to my room late at night to do this. One occurrence stands out in my memories very significantly as he was molesting me in the dark of my room in the night; I recall looking around the room and seeing what I realize now were demons. They were nasty, ugly creatures that encircled me and taunted me as my stepfather was holding me down. I remember feeling terrified and helpless. I also didn't quite understand what was happening to me when it came to the physical or sexual abuse. I knew it hurt, but I thought it was normal for other children.

The physical abuse consisted of intense beatings that commonly resulted in bruising and other injuries. I was beaten with belts while naked, thrown into walls, punched or kicked in the stomach, and much more. He also delighted in taunting me and making me flinch while we were in public. It was like he didn't ever want me to feel at peace or safe; he wanted me always to be afraid.

Around this time, my mother hired a new babysitter who often cared for us. She was probably in her 30s and had kids of her own. She would often babysit us at our house and bring her kids. Almost every time she came over, I was locked in a dark closet with my older sister. She would taunt and jeer at us from the outside and brag about how tasty the food she and her kids were eating was. Thankfully, this woman did not babysit us for more than two years.

School wasn't much of an escape. I was always rejected and picked on because I was different. I was born with a skin condition called piebaldism. It is a rare condition that most people have never heard of, but it is comparable to vitiligo. With both, you have areas of the skin that do not have any pigment at all. So, it makes you susceptible to sun damage as nothing protects you from the UV rays in these spots. The difference is that piebaldism is not progressive like vitiligo, and most people with piebaldism also end up with a white forelock (an area of hair at the front of the head with no pigment). The areas on my body affected are a spot on my forehead, both arms, my belly, and legs. The kids at school would see my skin, make fun of me, and run away, saying, "Don't touch her! She is diseased!"

With all these things happening, I commonly found comfort in escapism. I remember always using my imagination to leave my current reality and dream of a better place. The many hours I would spend locked away in my room waiting for my stepfather to enact the final stage of my punishment would be spent traveling to different far-off lands in my mind where I was someone who was loved and honored. The person I was in my daydreams was a hero who would save people when bad people were oppressing them. I also clung to a favorite stuffed animal that was another comfort source.

I do not remember receiving love or affection from any of my family members. My mother was not affectionate, nor did she tell me she loved me growing up. My memories of her from 6-10 were of her locked away in her bedroom or on the computer. She was always very distant.

Around the age of 6, we moved into a bigger and very nice house in a lovely suburb, complete with a huge backyard and pool. From the outside, our family seemed to have everything together.

It was around this time that my grandfather on my dad's side passed away. I was close to him and remember not understanding why he wouldn't return. Not too long after, my dad gave me up. At a court hearing for child support, he walked in and gave up his rights to me. At that point, my stepfather adopted me. The abuse from my stepfather continued and seemed to worsen. It continued until the age of 10 or 11. Things I was punished for, looking back now, seem outlandish. I remember one day, I was asked to wrap a game remote controller cord up (the old-school PS1), and because I was not doing it properly, my stepfather threw a large, heavy object at my eye, and I began to bleed.

There was a rule that I was not allowed to fall asleep anywhere but on my bed, and if I made the mistake of falling asleep on the couch, he would yell in my face.

I was also forced to constantly entertain and play with my younger sister- my stepfather's biological daughter. I would be punished if I did not do everything that she wanted me to do.

Most of my older sister's and my time at home outside of school was spent working endlessly on household chores. There was not much time for play.

My mother would also make these meals for just my older sister and me, which we did not like at all. My mom, stepdad, and little sister would be served something different that was more appetizing. I remember the meals often being so gross that I would gag as I attempted to eat them. My older sister and I would have to sit at the dining table until it was finished. If we didn't finish by bedtime, we would have to eat it for breakfast. Because of this, there were many times we didn't eat. It was around this age that I developed an unhealthy relationship with food. There were times at school when we had special holiday or pizza parties where I would eat as much as I possibly could and found extreme comfort in eating. Any opportunity I had to eat good food, I would almost gorge myself until I could barely move. One day, my teacher had leftover pizza after a pizza party and threw it in the trash. I immediately began crying and felt like I should have finished it myself.

Another rule at home was that if I wanted a drink of water, I would have to ask permission to get up and get water directly from a faucet in the bathroom. Cups were not allowed.

I remember many times my stepdad holding me over the open basement stairwell by my throat. There were also many times he put me outside on my front porch at night with the porch light on, completely naked. I remember being horrified and screaming, crying to come back in. I had 3 or 4 school friends living on that street, and I am unsure if they ever saw me. It was also typical to be thrown into and held down in a cold shower with all my clothes on. There were also many times I was placed in the corner overnight and fell asleep standing up.

The abuse took its toll on me, so much so that I attempted to run away around the age of 7 or 8. It was another day when I was sent to my room to await my stepdad's final punishment of beating or sexual abuse, and I was terrified. I removed the screen from my window, packed my pocket full of pennies, grabbed my stuffed dog on a leash, and bolted down the street to a friend's house. The cops eventually found me and brought me back home. I do not remember what happened that night once the police left, but I'm sure, given the severity of what I had done, it wasn't good.

The beatings were always very intense and often left bruising and cuts or scrapes on my body. One of the times that I was beaten and thrown into a wall, I was questioned at school. My teacher noticed the bruising and such and pulled me outside the classroom to ask what was happening. I told her the truth, and she reported it. That day, as I got off the school bus and walked inside my house, my mother said, "Sit down and tell us the lies you told everyone at school." I got in way more trouble than I had ever been. People from DFS and the school counselors were called to my school to talk to me. I was also made to return to school and report to DFS that I had lied about everything. Looking back, I don't know how they convinced me to do that.

It was also during this period that I struggled with sexual frustration and masturbation. I didn't understand where these impulses came from as a young child.

Occasionally, we would visit my grandma on my mom's side. She was married to my mom's stepdad, as my mom's parents had split at a young age. One particular evening we visited would be a life-altering moment. My grandmother and step-grandfather had separate rooms with separate beds. It was still early in the day, as plenty of sunlight came in through the windows, but my grandmother brought me into her husband's bedroom and told me to remove my bottoms and get into his bed. I asked her why I had to remove my bottoms because I was very uncomfortable, but she did not answer. She said I should remove them and put them in a drawer beside the bed. Not too long after, my step-grandfather later came into the room and sexually abused me.

Chapter 2

The Best of Times and the Worst of Times

One fine Friday, when I was about ten years old, a police officer knocked on the door and handed my mother a letter stating that we needed to be out of the house by the following Monday. I am unsure of all the details, but I was told it was due to my stepdad giving the house back to the bank. Complete chaos ensued as we hurriedly began to pack our entire house. My stepdad was away at work then, so my mother, older sister, and I were working as fast as possible. That evening, I remember my mother pulling my older sister aside to talk, and then my mom was in an uproar and called the police. My sister had told my mom how my stepdad was sexually abusing her. This came out when my mother asked my sister if things were happening... it wasn't the other way around. I will go deeper into that later. Not too long after, my stepdad pulled up and was arrested by the police. As I continued to pack up my things, I remember having a sense of peace as I knew I would no longer have to deal with the sexual, physical, mental, and emotional abuse of my stepdad.

The memories of the sexual abuse from my stepdad did not start coming back until I was a bit older, as I would blackout through most incidents. For this reason, I did not come out about the sexual abuse myself. Unfortunately, that did not matter because my mother knew what was happening to my older sister and me regarding the sexual abuse all the years she was with my stepdad and allowed it in the same way that she allowed and partook in the physical abuse.

During this time, we moved into my aunt's basement. Though I was relieved of being away from my stepfather, everything happening sent my body into a fit. My older sister and I were hospitalized for a week or so for high blood pressure and vomiting. Eventually, we could come home, but it wasn't long before my mother and aunt began fighting, and she kicked us out. My mother's father had taken in my stepdad and disowned my mother, so his house was not an option. My mother's other sister also cut ties, so the only place we had to go was the streets. We were without a place to live for quite a few months. Thankfully, several hotel and motel owners gave us a room during this period. I recall still going to school and having two outfits I would rotate, washing them in the sink with the complimentary shampoo and hanging them to dry over the room's AC unit. We would also walk to the restaurant next door for free water and hot cocoa. After some time, my mom began talking about this man she had met on the internet and how he would come to Missouri to meet us. Things moved quickly with my mom and this man as he rented a place for us, and we moved in with him.

My mother's relationship with this man was pretty rocky; there was much yelling when they were around. He would also yell at us kids, but thankfully, not much more than that. This period also began my mom's party lifestyle. She was typically gone, leaving us with my older sister. I did not have the best relationship with my older sister, as it was typical for her to bully me. She would also have friends over who would do the same. They would tell me how ugly I was and totally tear me apart. I believed them and didn't have too great of self-esteem. I was around 11 or 12, and no one taught me anything about personal hygiene or how to care for myself. I had pretty long hair that was always full of disgusting giant knots for which I would be made fun of at school. They were so bad that I had to cut some of them out. My wardrobe also consisted of clothes donated by churches and hand-me-downs that never fit correctly and were not "cool." So, that added to the reasons for being bullied at school. I had no friends until this girl in class started talking to me.

She was very kind to me, and I thought it was so nice of her to go out of her way to speak to me regardless of what the other kids said about me. She was rebellious, always loud in the hallways, and had many friends. She invited me to a sleepover at her house one evening, and my mom allowed me to go. Her parents allowed her and the other girls to drink alcohol. We also spent much of the night wrestling and goofing off. That was until her parents went to bed. Once her parents were gone, porn began to play on the giant big-screen tv. This was the first I had ever been introduced to this. I remember knowing it was bad, but I couldn't look away. We watched it until we all went to sleep. My friendship with this girl was eventually cut short as she was taken out of school due to some trouble she got into with some boys that she was having sex with.

During this time, I began to look at other females and be attracted to them. I had a few major crushes that I told no one about. That sort of thing was not accepted, so I kept it to myself. I was ashamed of it and saw it as something else that was wrong with me.

With instability and lack of peace everywhere I went, I turned my attention to video games. It was a great way to escape. I would spend all my free time playing these video games with my younger sister. This was the only time my younger sister and I would get along, as I typically yelled and lashed out at her in anger. I was always angry, but the video games provided comfort.

My mom's relationship with this man eventually ended, and we had to find a new place to live. My mom met another man who moved us into his three-bedroom trailer, where I shared a room with all three sisters.

Chapter 3

Far Gone

My mom's new relationship ended up being a good thing. This man cared very much about us kids and ensured we had food and any other needs he could provide. He was also very loving, played games with us, and cared about us. This was a change for me because it wasn't anything I had experienced previously. Though my mom's relationship with this new man was rocky, he was good to us kids. Things were okay for a while, but eventually, the fighting got worse, and my mom started disappearing more, leaving us with him. She was gone most of the weekends partying. At this point, I was around 12 years old.

At this stage, I still had no friends and was bullied at school. I began a new school every time we moved, but the kids always treated me the same. I was an outcast because of my skin, ratty clothes, and disheveled appearance. I was also a video game, cartoon, and hot wheel nerd, while all the girls in my school were into boy bands and name-brand clothes.

My mother and her boyfriend ended up breaking up after some time, but to my surprise, he moved out and allowed us to stay in his trailer because he did not want us to be homeless. This was very heartbreaking for me because I was losing the one father figure in my life who truly seemed to care for me. This also began the major party stage for my mom. She was gone every weekend, and it would sometimes go up to a week at a time when she was not coming back.

Because my mom was not working and had no one to provide for us, we rarely had food in the house. My mother had food stamps, but they always seemed to last for a week, and then we would scrounge for food for three weeks while we waited for the monthly supply of food stamps to be replenished. We also commonly went without power and water. We thankfully had two neighbors who would give us food and would even give us pots of hot water for baths and run over extension cords so that we could have power to a few items in the house. I also fondly remember eating cereal full of ants, complete with powdered milk. Cans of spam were also a staple food item during these times. We also found that my mom had a secret stash of snacks in her room that we would sneak little by little so that she did not notice.

My struggle with sexual frustration and masturbation also seemed to get worse. I lusted after many girls and boys in school but was usually too shy to speak to them. I also would wait until everyone was asleep to watch a channel that would slightly come in that had porn. It was an antennae TV, so I had to adjust it for this channel to come in.

When I hit 13, I began to change my interests and put more effort into my appearance to be accepted by other kids. I started playing with makeup and stealing my older sister's clothes to wear to school. She had a job at the mall and always bought the best name-brand clothes, so wearing those clothes made me a bit more accepted. In my first year of high school, I met a girl who quickly became one of my best friends. She felt terrible for me and often bought me lunch at school. She and her mother also took care of many needs I had.

This is also the year I had my first real boyfriend and began having sex. My mom was never home, so it was easy for me to sneak around. In the same year, I had a scare where the condom broke and I went to get a plan-b pill the next day, but that didn't stop me.

My mother had also never ceased in her practice of witchcraft. As a result, experiences of the supernatural were very common. My mom often would have friends over to play with Ouija boards and tarot cards. She was a self-proclaimed psychic and would encourage my sisters and me to use our own "psychic gifts." There were quite a few times she gave me tarot readings and would tell me that Mary (the mother of Jesus) often provided her with the information being shared in the cards. There was one day when we had a lot of demonic activity happening where my mom tried reciting a prayer, telling the entity to leave. The TV would turn static with every word she spoke, but only when she spoke. As she continued to walk around praying, pictures began falling off the walls, and objects flew off counters. There was also banging on the walls and front door. I frequently saw different entities around this house, both inside and out, that would take on the form of this woman in a white dress. I also often experienced watching drawers and doors opening right in front of my face, as well as "sleep paralysis." With every sleep paralysis incident, there was always a dark figure in the corner of the room.

It was common for us to have parties at the trailer since my mom was rarely home. This is when I was first introduced to marijuana and also began drinking heavily. I also gave myself over to more promiscuity. Though my boyfriend and I were off and on, I would still fool around with other boys that I partied with. There was one party that my friends brought me to where I was severely wasted. A random guy brought me into the woods and took advantage of me, and I did not fight him off. There was also another party I attended where I was very, very drunk and ended up being raped by a friend's family member, who was in his late 40s, after everyone had passed out.

My life continued to spiral more and more out of control as I continued to make bad decision after bad decision.

Chapter 4

Numb the Pain

As my high school years continued, I made friends who were more of the party scene, though I was still an outcast. The people I connected with were the ones considered to be the druggies. Other than that, I was the quiet, awkward kid. I hated most of my classes because none of my friends were there. I didn't know how to connect with people, nor did I try, as I was often rejected and was very socially awkward. I began smoking cigarettes more regularly, even stealing them from my mom's room while she was away. I would skip school often and rarely get caught because my mom was either gone or sleeping well into the afternoon, so she never took the school's calls. I would usually get high or drunk with friends. When I attended school, I didn't pay attention to my studies as I would skip most classes or sleep. I stopped caring so much that I flunked my freshman year. I dealt heavily with depression and anxiety and would often go to the counselor's office.

I found no comfort in any part of my life and was always trying to numb the depression and anxiety. I deeply desired to be loved and accepted, which I attempted to fulfill with boys. I thought if I found the right guy to love me, I would be fulfilled, and it would fix my problems. I was also easily pressured into fulfilling sexual favors and thought it was a requirement to receive love. Each time I gave myself away, that was usually the end of things, and it became this terrible cycle of heartbreak.

The toxic and abusive behavior from my mother continued and worsened the older I got. When I was younger, verbal abuse was more prevalent, but when I was in my teens, she became more physical. Any backtalking from my end resulted in her hitting and kicking me. One evening, she grabbed me by my hair and slammed my head into the stove, in which I ended up with a gash on my forehead. Most of my time spent with my mother at home resulted in me avoiding her and doing all the household chores that she required, including caring for my two younger sisters. My older sister had moved out to escape my mom by this time. I was not a very good caretaker of my little sisters because I spent most of my time angry and annoyed with them and hardly paid them any attention. When my mom was gone, I would have parties or invite friends over and always told them to play in their room.

My older sister would still visit when my mom was gone and invite friends to party. At this point, I began to connect with my older sister because we hung around some of the same people and were into the same things. One weekend, she invited me to a music festival called Schwagstock with some of our friends. It was unlike anything I had ever experienced. Upon arrival in the middle of the night, everyone was awake and partying. This place consisted of a sea of tents, huge fields with stages, and areas where hundreds of vendors sold various things. The roar of laughter, music, and liveliness echoed through the trees. I was amazed to see all these hippy people who were so loving and fun everywhere I looked. We soon made many friends who gave us ecstasy, and we walked about until the sun came up. As I walked around visiting with every single person I met, taking hits of different drugs, free hugs, and adventuring into various caves and cliffsides, I felt as though I had found where I belonged. We stayed awake for over 24 hours partying, taking drugs, listening to all of the musical artists, and adventuring and dancing until it was time to leave. Most of everyone the whole ride home was high, including the driver, so we scarcely made it back safe.

As soon as we got back, a deep depression hit me, unlike any I had experienced before. A mixture of coming off the drugs and leaving a place where I felt that I truly fit in deeply affected me, and I had to do anything to get back there. I went deeper into trying different types of drugs and drinking more and more. I was constantly chasing a high and a feeling that was never satisfied because it was never as good as the first time, no matter how much I took.

After a few years of my mom's ex allowing us to live in his trailer, he asked us to move out. My mother tracked my dad down during this time and asked if we could stay with him. He, of course, declined, but communication was open between him and me, and I was allowed to talk to him. He was still into the party life and women, so he didn't seem to have a major interest in coming back into my life, but we talked on the phone every now and then.

My mom ended up finding a place to live in the same school district through a housing program with the state. By this time, I was so focused on boys, getting to the next music festival, and getting high that I rarely attended school. I was also still very promiscuous and reached a point where I enjoyed juggling boys. I was receiving attention from many boys at one time and played with them, which resulted in hurting a few, but I didn't care. I liked having power over a boy and being able to make them like me, only to dump them soon after. If I was the one causing the breakup, I was free from the pain - so I thought.

During my junior year, I was working a job and began dating someone more seriously. One evening, I got into a severe fight with my mom and decided to move out. I moved right in with my boyfriend, who lived with three other guys that were in college. I also dropped out of school to work full-time to afford living expenses. This house was a full-on party house; there were seldom less than ten people visiting at a time, and drugs never ran dry. I began experimenting with more and more drugs, including different psychedelics and stimulants. I hated being sober and dealt with severe depression whenever I was. It was common for me to be high at work, too, either by popping pills or taking a bunch of shots before my shift. I have no idea how no one ever knew.

There was also a friend that I started hanging out with more and more during this period. He quickly became one of my best friends. He was different from all my other friends because he was very driven and sober, and he was in college. We would get into deep discussions about life, and he commonly shared the Gospel with me. I rejected the thought of a God who existed yet allowed me to go through the things I went through in my life. These conversations usually ended with me being angry, but it never strained our friendship because neither of us got terribly offended. However, it never stopped him from telling me about Jesus.

Some time passed while living in this party house, and eventually, we all got kicked out because we could not pay our rent. My boyfriend and I had to move in with my older sister, as we had nowhere to go. I later broke up with my boyfriend and started dating the man who would end up being my ex-husband.

Chapter 5

Desperately Searching for Love

The relationship with my ex-husband moved very fast. He taught me how to drive and helped me get my first car within a couple of months of us dating, and we moved in together three months later. Things seemed good initially, and we both fell for each other quickly. I remember feeling like I finally found someone that truly cared for me. This relationship was also the start of the most stable my life had ever been. I had food, a permanent place to live, my own vehicle, a steady job with a new promotion, and clothing that was actually mine and purchased new from a store. He also took an interest in the things I was into, like the music festivals, the drugs, and music, so we did everything together. After about 6 or 7 months in, we started having some pretty bad fights that ended in things being broken and even had some serious situations happen that the cops had to be called, but we stayed together.

It wasn't long after things started to get difficult between us that I found out I was pregnant. By this time, I had been speaking to my dad by phone more often and called to tell him the news. He totally lost it, which I couldn't understand. Because he had given me up at the age of 6 and was hardly in my life, more focused on partying and hanging out with his biker buddies. While on the phone with him, he threatened to come and kill my ex-husband for getting me pregnant. I was terrified because I knew my dad's past. We immediately packed up some things and went to stay at my sister's house. After a day of staying out at my sister's, I began to spot. We went to the hospital right away, and the doctors told me the baby would be fine and sent me home. A few nights later, I woke up in the most pain I had ever been in my life; I went to the bathroom and found I was bleeding profusely. I was rushed to the hospital and ended up passing out as I walked into the E.R. The doctors came in and told me that I was miscarrying the baby. I was devastated.

After being in the hospital for a day or so, they sent me home and informed me that I had not passed all of the remains of the baby and that I would have to collect them as they passed and bring them to my doctor to ensure that everything had come out. Otherwise, they would have to do a D&C to remove anything that had not passed on its own. This was absolutely traumatic; all I could do was scream and cry every time I passed some of the baby's remains. Thankfully, my ex-husband was right there with me through this and helped with everything. I ended up not needing the procedure because my body was able to pass everything naturally.

I went into a deep depression after this and stopped talking to my dad. I blamed him for the miscarriage because the doctors said it could have been brought on by stress. Most days, I spent sleeping in my bed, and I also didn't want anything to do with sex anymore because I was scared of the same thing happening again. I also developed an addiction to the pain pills that I was on after the miscarriage and started buying them from friends off and on after I ran out of my prescription. This went on for quite a few months before I started to come out of it.

We continued the party lifestyle and went to music festivals whenever we could. We drank and did whatever party drugs we could get a hold of every weekend and sometimes during the week. We often had parties at our apartment. I still struggled with my attraction to women and often took advantage of this while partying. My ex-husband did not mind my involvement with women as long as he was not left out.

We ended up getting engaged and started planning for our wedding. I had second thoughts about the marriage because of our fights, but I pushed them away and convinced myself everything would be okay. As we were planning for the wedding, I ended up getting pregnant again. Because of this, we had to cancel all previous plans and move the date up; otherwise, I would have been eight months pregnant during the ceremony.

I was married at the age of 19 and had my son at 20 years old. I was ecstatic to be a mother, and my son was the most beautiful thing I had ever seen. I had a C-section due to how large he was; my doctor said his shoulders were too wide for the birth canal. Upon arriving home, I began to deal with the most intense anxiety I had thus far in life. The depression and anxiety I was already experiencing most of my life seemed to increase 100-fold. I had the most irrational fears I had ever experienced. I was afraid to leave the house with my son, thinking we would be in a car crash or some crazy sickness would take him. I would obsessively watch over him to make sure he was breathing. I could never shut off my mind and stop these horrific images and scenarios from coming in. I let my doctor know what was going on, and he diagnosed me with postpartum depression. I was put on medication that seemed only to make it worse. I eventually stopped the medication, but it never seemed to get better.

Having a son did not stop me from partying, going to music festivals, or drinking and drugs. It just required us to get a sitter to go and have fun. By this time, I was in complete turmoil inside due to ever-increasing anxiety and depression, and I was not happy with my relationship. The fighting got worse and worse, and I did not have much freedom. If I wanted to spend even a dollar at my work vending machine, I would have to call and ask. If I ever wanted to go hang out with friends, I usually was not allowed to. We continued to do everything together; we rarely left each other's side. The only time we spent apart was at work. I also continued struggling with my attraction to women in, which he still allowed me to be involved with women as long as he was not left out.

I found out I was pregnant with my daughter about a year after my son. I hated the pregnancies because I dealt with many different health issues, and I was forced into being sober and dealing with my own thoughts and feelings, but it was always worth it in the end. Becoming a mother of my beautiful baby girl was one of the best days of my life. She looked exactly like me upon arrival; she even had the same birthmark, complete with an awesome white forelock of hair. I unfortunately was dealing with the same postpartum depression, but I was determined to push through it.

After a week of being home, we were sitting in the backyard with company that came to visit. I heard my daughter coughing on the baby monitor, so I went inside to check on her. As I walked over to her, I noticed that she was turning blue and not breathing; I immediately panicked and started screaming for help. Everyone came inside and called 911. The ambulance got there within 3 minutes and was able to get her to take some breaths, but she was still having a lot of trouble. They put her in the back of the ambulance and only allowed me to ride in the back with her. As we made our way to the hospital, weaving in and out of traffic with the sirens going, I began to do the only thing I knew. I attempted to bargain with the God I didn't believe in and said my first "prayer." I told Him, "If you let her live, I'll live right and start going to church!".

As we were getting out of the ambulance, my ex-husband asked me what was all over my face and body. I looked in the mirror and saw that I was completely covered in hives from fear. The doctors were able to regulate her breathing and told us that they wanted her to be seen by a special children's hospital. While there, she was diagnosed with reflux. The doctors said she would have to be propped up and closely monitored after every meal to ensure she would not suffocate on the large amounts of vomit that would sometimes occur. I was so thankful she would be okay and just as quickly forgot about my promise to the "non-existent God,"... but He sure didn't.

My life continued on down the destructive path as my depression and anxiety got even worse. By this time, I could barely leave the house on my own because of irrational fears. I only went to work and back. I couldn't even go to grocery stores by myself. Anytime I was in public, I became terrified of social situations. When anyone would pay attention to or speak to me, my whole body would begin to tremble. I couldn't even make eye contact with co-workers. I had frequent panic attacks where I thought I was dying. My chest and airways would tighten, and I would feel as though I couldn't breathe. This would happen multiple times a day. The only thing that would make me feel somewhat normal was popping pills or taking shots of alcohol, so I spent much of my time numbing myself with substances to get through my day. I would often take a few shots early in the morning before going to work, and I would often get pills from co-workers.

I felt so worthless as a mother because I couldn't take them to do things, and I was easily stressed and upset. The fighting with my ex-husband continued to get even worse, and we barely got along. I felt trapped in a prison of fear and believed I was more of a burden than anything good to anyone in my life. I began to listen to the overwhelming thoughts and feelings of worthlessness and shame and began contemplating taking my life. I believed that I caused more harm than good and that everyone would be better off. I started to plan how I would do it, as I wanted it to be easy for everyone in my life. I thought about using a gun to either shoot myself in the head or the stomach but figured that would be too messy, so I decided it would be best to take an entire bottle of pills that I had in my medicine cabinet.

As I was secretly planning my suicide, God had different plans.

Chapter 6

New Beginnings

One day at my job, we had some other women from different departments brought in to help with an overload of work that we had to complete. One of these women, Tyesha, was put right by me. She was talking to the other girls around us about different things, and we got on the subject of God. During the conversation, I made fun of her because she had mentioned she doesn't drink or watch certain movies and such, but she wasn't fazed by it. She began talking about her relationship with Jesus and how He talks to her. At this point, I was completely enamored. I had never heard anything like this before. I had no idea that we could have an actual relationship with God and that it wasn't all about following a set of rules. I began to ask her a bunch of questions, and by the end of the day, she had invited me to church.

I accepted Tyesha's invitation to church on a Wednesday evening, which was a pretty big deal, considering I never went anywhere by myself because of my major anxiety issues. I picked her up on the way, and as we walked in, the service had already started. I quickly notice that I am the only white person in the building, and I am a bit taken aback by everyone jumping and waving their hands.

As I walk down the aisle to a seat, the woman preaching at the front points to me and starts talking all about my life. As she speaks about things only God could have known, I end up in the front of the church, and she touches the top of my head. I immediately fell under the power of God. In this moment, I saw God for who He is and saw just how sinful I was. It's like everything I ever did flashed before my eyes, and I laid on the floor weeping, saying, "I'm so sorry" over and over again. His presence was so strong and full of peace; it was like He wrapped me in a blanket on that floor.

After quite some time, I was able to get up and take a seat near my friend. I immediately noticed the absence of fearful, irrational thoughts and thought about everything that had just happened. I looked over at my friend and said, "What the &%$@ just happened?! (Jesus hadn't yet cleaned up my language).

They continued praying and preaching well into the night, and I had zero desire to leave. His presence was so tangible I could have stayed there forever. I made the decision that night that I wanted Jesus. As we left, I went to light a cigarette before getting into the vehicle and heard a voice say, "You don't need that anymore." I put out the cigarette I lit and threw the rest away. I knew the Lord had taken that addiction from me.

After arriving home, I told my husband everything that had happened, and he thought I was absolutely insane. I didn't care because I knew what happened was real and was excited about my newfound relationship. After a few days, I noticed that my overwhelming desire to end my life was completely gone. Jesus saved me right before I made a decision to take my life and spend eternity in hell. He took the irrational fears and started to deliver me from my addictions little by little. I still fought the panic attacks and anxiety, but it was nowhere near as intense as it was previously. The Lord began teaching me to lean on Him and study His word.

At the same time, I began to have some memories of the sexual abuse from my childhood come back. I had blocked many of them from my memory, and the devil began to make me remember certain scenarios to drive me away from the Lord. I also began to get very sick and struggle with many different health ailments. The Lord strengthened me, and I was able to press on despite the heavy spiritual attack. I ended up getting baptized two months after I gave my life to Christ.

The strain on my marriage became more apparent than ever. As the Lord began to heal me and remove my fears, I became less weak and desired some normalcy. I desired to go to church and hang out with friends, but my ex-husband did not like that. We continued to fight constantly, and there was rarely peace in the home. My ex had a very short temper, so if the smallest of things went wrong in the home, it would set him off. We rarely went a day without him yelling at everyone. I was not without blame because I did not back down from all the yelling and arguments and choose the way of peace. I could have spent more time praying for him instead of engaging in and getting sucked into the arguments. As I continued growing in the Lord and coming out of my fears, it caused even more arguing because he couldn't control everything I did as easily anymore. Before I got saved, I was always home because I was terrified of everything, but now that I was being set free, he didn't like that I was making friends and wanting to have a somewhat normal social life.

I continued seeking the Lord and even began asking the Lord to baptize me with His Holy Spirit. I knew what the Bible said about needing the power of the Holy Spirit to walk out your calling here on the earth and sought after the baptism of the Holy Spirit earnestly. After being saved for about nine months, my pastor called me up to the front of the church and said he wanted to pray for me to receive the baptism of the Holy Spirit. He told me to begin thanking the Lord, so I did. At that moment, I felt the power of God come over me, and the English words that I was speaking quickly changed to another unknown language. I fell out under the power of the Holy Spirit and continued speaking in this unknown tongue.

Life was truly amazing at this point. I was growing in my relationship with Christ and began hearing His voice. He would wake me up most mornings around 5 am to go pray by filling my room with His presence so tangibly that I would wake up. I would sit with Him for an hour or so, reading my Bible and praying, being sure to write down everything He told me in a journal. I also began to get so many prophetic words from the Lord about His plans for my life. He would confirm these words by having many different people speak the same thing to me. He began to tell me that I am an evangelist and that I would have my own street ministry. He told me that I would speak in front of many different people of all different backgrounds and nationalities and that I would be in front of crowds of people confidently speaking, praying, prophesying, etc. As I began to receive these words, I became afraid because I didn't know how I could possibly do any of this. I was someone who was afraid of having the attention of more than one person on me; how could I ever get up on a stage?

My ex-husband and I's relationship was extremely strained at this point. The fighting was constant, and he didn't want much to do with me. It was so bad that he constantly told me how he didn't even know who I was anymore. I begged him to go to marriage counseling with me, but he refused. He also did not like coming to church with me because he said he was uncomfortable with us being the only white people there. I began looking for a church that he would be more comfortable with in hopes that God would change his life as well. That eventually fell through, and we stopped going to the new church. I had started going to college full-time, so I didn't have a ton of free time to make it to service every weekend.

I continued to seek after the Lord, but no longer being connected to the body of Christ made it difficult. At this point, my ex-husband was drinking a lot more often and acting out in anger much more. I began to feel like I couldn't take it anymore. I would weigh what was worse, keeping my kids in an unstable environment for the sake of the marriage or getting a divorce. I eventually came to him and told him that I wanted a divorce. At that moment, his behavior totally changed. He told me he was willing to do whatever it took to fix things between us and scheduled a marriage counseling session with a pastor. He also began doing thoughtful things like leaving me notes and buying me flowers. There was so much peace in the home, and the kids were very happy. I couldn't believe how much he had changed; he was a totally new person. The yelling and anger completely stopped. I pushed off the idea of getting a divorce since things were finally working out.

Chapter 7

When the Enemy Comes in Like a Flood

Things were going well for about six months, and suddenly, all of my ex-husband's old behavior came back, and our home life returned to how it used to be. It was back to constant yelling and arguments and walking on eggshells. I felt like I had been tricked. I had enough at this point and couldn't take the instability. I told him I wanted a divorce for real this time. He tried to convince me otherwise, but my mind was made up. We separated, and he moved out of our house after a couple of months, and we were divorced a few months later.

At this point, I was completely overcome with guilt and condemnation. I felt selfish for making the call to separate my family, and being separated from the body of Christ allowed the enemy to come in like a flood and convince me to walk away from my Father. I believed the lies that I was condemned because I was divorced. Being totally and completely overcome by guilt and condemnation, I gave up on my walk with Christ and went full-on back into the world.

I began getting on dating apps and meeting all different kinds of people, including men and women, drinking, doing drugs, partying, and seeking after pleasure. Around this time, I also began to struggle with a porn and masturbation addiction. This was something I took part in daily, sometimes multiple times a day, no matter how disgusting it made me feel.

I also began working two jobs because my current career as a veterinary technician couldn't sustain me as a single mother, so I also became a server. Because of this, I hardly saw my kids, which was terrible because they were already dealing with the divorce and splitting their time with both parents. During this time, I also began to shut down emotionally with them. I felt terrible for hurting them by divorcing their father, and it was as if I put up this wall with them. As if I no longer deserved their love and adoration. It also didn't help that their father was bitter toward me for the divorce and convinced them that it was all my fault and that I was the reason for the divorce. So, due to my own selfishness and the working of their father to turn the kids against me, my relationship with them became very, very strained.

A few months after the divorce, I went out with friends one night. I had worked 16 hours the day before, got about 4 hours of sleep, and worked an 8-hour shift that day. I had been drinking but was smart enough to space it out before my drive home that night. As I was driving home in my Jeep Wrangler without a seatbelt at about 60mph on a country backroad, I fell asleep at the wheel. I went into a ditch and flipped it 3 or 4 times. I had nodded off for just a moment and opened my eyes right as I started to go into the ditch. I then blacked out into the first flip. The next thing I remember, I am standing on the outside of my Jeep, looking at it as it's lying on its side with the roof completely ripped off. I should have died that day. I should have flown out of my Jeep and been crushed. But God, in His mercy, sent an angel to save me, even while I was deep in my sin, and turned my back on Him.

I recognized that He had saved me, but I still hardened my heart toward Him. I went deeper and deeper into trying to distract myself and cover up the pain, all while pretending like God didn't exist even though I knew without a doubt that He did. During the times that the kids were with their father, I was a loose cannon. I was doing all kinds of drugs, drinking heavily, going out to clubs, and sleeping around. This went on for quite a few years, and not much changed. I thought about the Lord every day, but I was too stubborn to go back.

I had thought I tried His way, and it didn't work. But I was wrong. Somewhere along the way, I got caught up in religion, and it became more about what I could do than what Jesus did for me. See, I hadn't yet experienced the transformational love of my Father that would lead me out of my pit. This is why I was deceived, and it was so easy for me to make the decision to walk away from Him.

Chapter 8

Prodigal Come Home

My party lifestyle began to slow down as I got into a serious relationship with a man. After a while, my kids met him, and we moved in together. Things were looking up as stability and structure returned to my family, or so I thought. After 6 months of living together, things began to take a dark turn. He became verbally and mentally abusive. I couldn't tell at the time, but he was trying to tear me down to nothing in order to shape me into what he wanted me to be, all while controlling everything that I was. At the time, I was totally blind to what was happening and believed he loved me. I thought he was just struggling with insecurities in himself and that one day, we would work it all out. He would often lash out in anger and then twist it to make me believe I was the problem, which I often believed. This went on for some time until it eventually began to turn physically abusive. There were one or two instances where I was thrown down to the ground or shoved, but I would just brush it off. He ended up proposing on Christmas, and I hesitantly said yes.

I began to sink into a deep, deep depression that nothing could pull me out of. I felt trapped because I didn't want to hurt my children by separating them from another man that they cared about. I couldn't hurt them again. As I sunk into despair and depression, I began to want to take my life again. I felt like there was no way out. I was completely shut down to everyone, including my children. This was during the events of 2020, in which there was much time spent at home because of the lockdowns. I began to escape more and more into video games during this time as it was one of the only ways I had to cope. I ended up being introduced to friends in a game one day with whom I had a lot in common. One of them was a girl who lived in Bermuda. We would get into deep discussions about Jesus because we both had encountered Him and had many awesome stories to share with each other.

Fast forward almost a year, and my friend from Bermuda came to visit for a few days. We finally got to meet in person after only ever gaming together. During her time here, we really connected and had a great time, but the enemy also tried to pervert our friendship. The Lord was using her to speak into my life and draw me back to Himself. But the devil was also there trying to tear down what was happening. On the last day I had with her, the Holy Spirit showed up in our conversation, and we began to cry as we discussed serious things while sitting on a beach at a lake. It was in this conversation I knew I had to get out of the relationship I was in.

Then, three days later, after a long day of work, my ex-fiancé came into my office angry because I used an old kitchen towel to detail my vehicle. The verbal altercation quickly turned physical, and before I knew it, everything in my office had been totally trashed, and I was on the floor. Something came over me, and I fought back and threatened to call the cops. He retreated, and I picked myself off the floor to call the father of my kids. I knew that if I told him, I would never be able to stay in this relationship because he would not allow me to keep the kids in danger. The craziest thing about everything that occurred that day is the fact that the day I got engaged, my ex-fiancé called all of his family in India to tell them we were getting married in 6 months (even though I was hesitant). This was because it was common in his culture to be married within six months of engagement. Well, the day he physically assaulted me was exactly six months to the day of our engagement. In which we ended up broken up instead of married.

My life took a quick turn as I saw the Lord trying to get my attention even in my deep darkness. My heart began to soften toward the Lord again, and I had a desire to seek Him. My friend from Bermuda ended up moving in with me, and we began searching for a church. We found one via the internet that we wanted to try out and made plans to go the very next weekend.

The day before church, I took my Jeep through a carwash in which the main roller smashed through my windshield, and my kids and I were trapped inside. That left me without a vehicle, and we were not able to go to church until a few weeks later.

It's so funny looking back and seeing not only God's hand but also the devil's. Anytime I made efforts to seek after God, all hell would break loose in my life. Every single time without fail. The devil always overplays his hand. So if you are at a place of surrendering to the Lord for the first time or returning back to Him and you begin to see everything going wrong, submit to God, resist the devil, and he will flee. When we go to the Lord, we become an enemy of satan, who is the god of this world, and he will cause bad things to happen in order to make you run in fear or even believe it is God causing it.

We are in a spiritual war, and when we surrender to the Lord, we join the ranks of the Lord's army. The enemy may form weapons, but they will not prosper. Take heart because Jesus has already overcome the world.

Chapter 9

Begin Again

After my friend and I joined this new church, I also joined a discipleship program and began to grow quickly in the Lord. Though I hadn't quite let go of the world, the Lord was doing a great work in my heart. One day at church, the Holy Spirit convicted my heart of not forgiving my mother and father for things that they did in the past. I had already been confessing that I forgave them, but the Lord showed me that there was still pain, bitterness, and unforgiveness in my heart toward them. I brought it up to the altar that day, and someone prayed for me.

I was so used to feeling my stomach drop or stressed when anyone would bring up my mother due to her lifestyle. Even at the time of writing this, she is still living on the streets and battling her drug addiction. So when someone mentions her name, I would feel worry and a rush of other emotions because you just never know if you will hear of her being found not alive; even old memories would pop up.

Well, a couple of weeks after I had gone up for prayer, I was working and had a thought of my mother come into my mind. Instead of the usual gut-wrenching feeling, what filled my heart was this supernatural, unconditional love. I began to weep uncontrollably as I realized God had completely healed my heart of all the pain my mother had caused and filled it with love for her. All it took was for me to repent of the unforgiveness and ask His help to forgive her, and He picked up where I couldn't. He continued to do this for me concerning many other people I hadn't truly forgiven.

If there is anyone that comes to mind as I share this with you, I encourage you to go to the Lord with it. Someone may have done something to you that is so atrocious and doesn't deserve forgiveness, but the Bible is clear. If we don't forgive others, He won't forgive us. There is no exception, no matter how terrible the atrocity done against you. We must be willing to forgive as Jesus has forgiven us for all the terrible things we ourselves have done. Just go to the Lord and ask Him to help you to forgive and heal those broken places of your heart.

As I began to heal and grow, I went to the Lord in prayer one day and told Him that I only wanted the man He had for me.

The moment I confessed this out loud, I suddenly had men coming from every which way, hitting on me and asking me out. I kid you not. I had 30-plus friend requests coming in on social media per day, all from single men. I was not on any dating apps or anything either, as I was serious about the Lord. Many of them were professing Christians, but I quickly learned the hard way that just wasn't so by them not being okay with me not wanting any sort of physical contact. Unfortunately, I ended up getting distracted by a couple of them and getting thrown off my walk, but the Lord was merciful.

It was around this time I met Jason. We began talking after he reached out to me on social media. In one of our very first phone conversations, he let me know that he did not plan on dating anyone as he was setting aside three months with the Lord to consecrate and seek Him. To which I replied, "Good for you, buddy, but that's quite the assumption.." We agreed to meet in person after about one month of talking. He came to pick me up at my house, and I remember looking at the large clock on my wall before I walked out my front door. It was January 30th at exactly 3:14 pm. I knew that was the exact moment because he sent me a text when he arrived. It was at that very moment that the large clock on my wall stopped working right at 3:14 pm. I later ended up throwing it away because it didn't work anymore.

Our conversations were filled with the things of God as we drove around talking. One of the most significant things we discussed was why we don't see the Book of Acts happening today and how dead the American church is. We ended up grabbing a bite to eat as well but kept it casual as we were both serious about not dating. I remember having many walls up toward him and not being attracted to him initially. I believe that was the protection of the Lord because he is the hottest thing I've ever seen.

About two weeks later, as we continued talking, he told me that he was asking God about me because he was worried that I might be a distraction from his relationship with the Lord. He told me God responded with:

"Pray and intercede for her; don't let your flesh get in the way. Both of you aren't ready; I am not finished. I desire your hearts fully; let me fill the cup with the wine that I started to fill. When I am finished, I will let you drink of the cup I'm preparing. The wine isn't fermented and will taste good to the tongue but will mess up your tummies. Let it go through the time, the fire; let Me stomp out the grapes in your lives; let Me pull out the bugs and bitter leaves. I will fill your cup so you may drink new wine that no one else I will allow to drink, and when you're done drinking, I will personally break the cup."

As soon as Jason told me this, I shut down and thought he was insane because I understood the symbolism behind this word. See, I knew that in Jewish wedding ceremonies, the man and woman both drink wine from a cup and then it is thrown to the ground and broken. I ended up kind of pushing him away, but at the same time, I started to ask God about Jason.

One morning in prayer, as I was asking God about Jason, He took me into a vision of about six past moments where I was crying out to the Lord for a true man of God. In this vision, I felt every single emotion I had felt in those very moments all over again.

Then, there was one night when Jason and I stayed up talking on the phone for about 9 hours. During this conversation, Jason opened up to me about pretty much his whole life, and I was still very closed off and had up many walls. All of a sudden, out of Jason's mouth came all of these things about me, things I had been through in the past, many of which I had never told anyone. As he began to tell me all these things about my life, my jaw dropped, and I instantly became offended at God and almost hung up on Jason. I was offended at God because I knew Jason only knew what he knew because God told him. The next day, the Holy Spirit began to work on my heart and let me know that He would never share those things with Jason if I couldn't trust him. This was the beginning of me letting my walls down with Jason. God had to nudge me into opening up to him. Because I now knew that God was leading me in that direction, I was later able to open up to him, unlike I had to anyone else.

A few weeks later, while I was spending time in prayer, God randomly spoke to me the dates 6/11 through 6/19. When He said this, I was a bit confused, so I looked at my calendar on my phone. I realized the 11th was a Saturday. When I saw this, it was like I suddenly knew that God was telling me that it was the day of my wedding and the week after was my honeymoon. I believed it so much that I requested the days off of work immediately. Then I went to Jason and told him that God had given me the date and that I would not be telling him the day, month, or year. I explained to him that unless God confirmed the date with him, it wasn't going to happen. Prior to me saying this to him, he was hearing God speak so clearly every morning. But as soon as he began to ask God for the date, He went silent.

I began to get nervous at this point because the wedding was supposed to happen in just a few months, but now God was quiet. About 6 or 7 weeks later, Jason and I were praying together after church. Jason was praying about something random, not even concerning the wedding, and suddenly, at the end of his sentence, out of his mouth comes "6/11". I was silent for a moment and then said, "W-w-what did you just say?" To which he replied, "Uh, I don't know... 6/11?" I then screamed, "THAT'S THE DAY!!!" We both immediately began to cry as we knew God was 100% in this. The best thing about it was I had the proof that he spoke out of his mouth the correct date because I had already requested off of work.

We got straight to wedding planning and noticed that we kept hearing and seeing Zion everywhere, so we began to ask God if He wanted us to get married there. We also considered having a small outdoor wedding at a state park or something since most venues were booked out due to the influx of ceremonies that were postponed during the 2020 shutdowns.

As we were praying one day, asking God about the venue, I suddenly saw a vision of this beautiful orangish wood cabin near a lake. I described it to Jason, and he said, "I know exactly where that is!". He made a phone call, and we ended up setting up a meeting to look at this venue at a place called Redemption Ranch. The wedding venue itself was booked out for two years, but the Ranch had a ton of land with a cabin that was open for use the day of the wedding. As we pulled up, I quickly realized it was the exact cabin I had seen in the vision, with the lake right next to it. There was also a giant cross in the field next to the cabin, so we figured we could get married at the cross and have a small reception of 30 people afterward at the cabin. We spoke to the owner about it, and she agreed that it would be a great idea.

Instead of paying, she asked if we would tile a shower for her as Jason owns his own construction company. We thought that was a great deal and agreed. As we drove back from viewing the venue that night with my maid of honor, Jason was in the backseat, and he said the Holy Spirit came upon him so strong and told him, "Samantha is my daughter, and I am going to pay for her wedding."

About a week later, after we finished tiling her shower, Jason went to send her a text asking a few questions about tablecloths and chairs. Before he could hit send, she sent him a text saying they had originally had the main event wedding venue set aside for a pastor's convention, but they wanted us to have it AND at no additional cost!! I fell to my knees in thankfulness when Jason told me because I was totally in awe of God's goodness.

Immediately after that, friends and family started coming from everywhere asking to help us with planning and even took care of the catering with a full menu and everything. One of my closest friends even offered to help me plan the wedding, all while facing divorce herself.

One of the most significant changes in my heart was a desire to wear a wedding dress. See, I had never really owned a dress nor desired to. I had only ever worn dresses at other people's weddings as a bridesmaid (because I had no choice). At my first wedding, I even wore pants and a dress shirt. My whole life, I have never been super girly. I grew up playing with Hot Wheels and bugs. I thought dresses and dolls were silly. As I got older, I would wear makeup, but my wardrobe always consisted of jeans and a t-shirt or hoodie. I commonly shopped in the men's section because I like the fit of men's clothing better. Suddenly, I noticed different dresses and skirts were catching my eye, especially ones that were lavender or light purple. Then, the repulsion toward a wedding dress dissipated, and I knew that I needed to at least go and try some on. I ended up finding the perfect dress and couldn't believe it. Not long after I picked my wedding dress, I began to fill my closet with many skirts and dresses.

As the planning continued, Jason and I began to plan for the future and discuss where we would live after we were married. We decided my house would be the better option. Since he had purchased his home about two years prior, he went to go look at the paperwork to see when he could sell his house to avoid capital gains tax. Where we live, if you sell a house in under two years of purchase, you are required to pay 30% capital gains, and we definitely wanted to avoid that. Upon finding the paperwork, he discovered that he had bought the house on 6/11, exactly two years prior. We laughed and laughed because God was just confirming the date with us left and right.

The wedding happened on 6/11 as planned, and it was the most beautiful ceremony filled with the presence of the Lord. We ended up honeymooning at Zion National Park, and it was a truly unforgettable experience.

Chapter 10

Scales Removed

We settled in as newlyweds quickly, and our families blended fairly well, considering how fast everything happened. The month after Jason and I were married, we went on a trip with a couple of friends to Glacier National Park. On our last day of the trip, we were able to head to the point of the highest elevation to hike, as it was previously closed due to snow on the road. As we began our hike up the mountain, everyone else was headed down due to an incoming storm. The lightning was so intense that our hair was sticking straight up, and it was raining, so it was quite slippery walking on the snow. The rain, slippery snow, lightning, and fresh bear tracks in the snow made for quite a dangerous trek, but we didn't care because we had waited all week to be able to do this hike. We reached a point on the trail where there was a stretch of 3ft wide path with an almost straight drop off to the left, and on the right, there was an upward slope. Our friends chose to take a longer but less dangerous way to our destination at the top of the mountain, while Jason and I chose to stay on the path.

As we were hiking the most dangerous part of the path, I made the mistake of looking to my left. Just as I spoke, "I just looked down." My foot slipped on the snow, and I began to slide to the left. Jason immediately grabbed my hands in an attempt to stop me from going over the edge, but it was too late. He knew he couldn't stop me, so he went with me. He somehow put himself in a position where he was underneath me, sliding on his back as I was on his lap, clawing at the side of the mountain with my hand and digging my knees and feet into the snow in an attempt to stop us from falling. We fell about 600 yards before we came to a stop. See, if Jason hadn't thrown himself down with me, I would have either ended up dead or severely injured because of the way in which I was falling. God used this very moment to show me that I could trust Jason with my everything. Any walls or doubt I had as far as trusting Jason were completely shattered in that moment. As we headed down the mountain, a beautiful rainbow appeared.

Life was quiet for the next few months as we continued to settle into our new routines. Along with being married and moving in together, we had decided to work together as well. Jason had his own construction company, and I ended up leaving my job to work with him. Things became very difficult during this time as many things began to stir up in both of us. Going from being independent to spending every waking moment with someone is a very significant change. When we are living for ourselves, we will not see negative things inside of us that lie dormant. But the moment you enter into marriage and lay your life down for the other person, things begin to come up that you never knew existed. I believe this is one of the Lord's main purposes for marriage. He uses it as a tool for sanctification.

After about four months of us being married, I began to feel very convicted with how I was living. Even though I was spending time with the Lord in prayer daily, reading my Bible, and going to church, I felt so deeply that I was not doing what I was supposed to be doing. It was then that the Lord revealed to me that I had not surrendered every part of my life to Him. He showed me that I was still holding onto dreams and goals that were not His will for my life.

I also had many vices and worldly habits that were not pleasing to Him. He also began to remind me of my calling and showed me that I was hiding behind "religious duties" to avoid actually fully surrendering to Him. I had a relationship with Him, knew His voice, and experienced His presence every day in the secret place, but that was that. I wouldn't step out of the boat into the deep; I was playing it safe. He also began to show me how selfish I was. I was hoarding the Gospel and keeping it all to myself, having a good time in the world and laughing as many around me were headed straight to hell.

The conviction became so strong that I began to express it to Jason. The Lord was simultaneously working on his heart and convicting him of the same. We both began to understand that Jesus didn't die for us to live a complacent life of churchgoing, Bible studies, and prayer, all while fulfilling the American dream.

Jesus saved us, but we had allowed the enemy to deceive us with religion. We were deceived into checking off our boxes of religious duties in order to avoid our God-given callings that were established before the foundations of the earth. The Lord began to show us both that we were worldly, carnal Christians who were lukewarm and had a form of godliness but denied His power. That was terrifying to us because we all know what Jesus said He would do with lukewarm Christians – spit them out of His mouth.

I began to study evangelism and even shared some things with my pastors. When I spoke to them about this, the main scripture I shared around was Mark 16: 15-18. It's funny because, at the time, it had totally gone over my head what Jesus was saying would be signs that would follow a true believer. The first sign mentioned was casting out demons – which I had never seen anyone do, nor had I done it myself. I had never even thought about demons before.

Fast forward a couple of weeks later, I was scrolling on social media and saw a friend post a video of a Christian having a demon cast out of them. I was mind blown by what I saw because you could definitely tell this was real, and also, I couldn't believe this was a Christian.

I then went into more research on this and began to question all of my theology. Why was I totally blind to deliverance? Why did I believe once you were saved, it was not possible to have a demon? As I scoured all of the Gospels over and over, I found that deliverance was 1/3 of Jesus' ministry. He went from synagogue to synagogue casting out demons, and often, in order for someone to receive healing, an infirmity spirit needed to be cast out. He also told us to cast out demons, not pray them away.

I also found that the Greek word that was translated to possessed in the KJV is daimonizomai, which better translates to under the power of a demon or demonized. The word possessed makes it seem as though we are owned by the devil and is, in my opinion, an incorrect translation. We can be under the power of a demon and not owned by it.

I also saw that Jesus referred to deliverance as "the children's bread" and pointed out that if an unclean spirit goes out of a man's soul (house) and comes back to find it empty, it will get seven more spirits more wicked than itself and occupy that place again.

As Jason and I dug deeper and deeper to search for the truth, we began to have more supernatural experiences. Before this, we had experienced the presence of God, but now, other things were beginning to reveal themselves. One day, as I was sitting in my living room, I felt an evil presence enter, along with the most horrendous stench you could ever imagine. The best way to describe it is sulfur and 1,000-year-old rotten eggs. At that moment, I was also gripped with an indescribable fear. Along with constant nightmares and other experiences like this, it seemed as though this was our new normal.

The reason why these things were revealing themselves was to instill fear and keep us from finding the truth. The Lord was also revealing things to us that were inside of us that needed to go. He began to show me that because I was filled with His Holy Spirit, I had a fruit of self-control. So, I wasn't totally under the power of these things while I was walking in His Spirit. But He reminded me of times when I would be going through a difficult period where I would get in my flesh, which would give way to these unclean spirits to torment me. He reminded me of times when I would suddenly have extreme thoughts and impulses to do things that I had believed I no longer struggled with, like suicide, depression, anxiety, rage, and many other things.

He also began convicting us of things we allowed in our lives and homes that were displeasing to Him. He told Jason to dump his bourbon collection and told me to dump my wine.

We would only ever have a glass at a time and never be drunk, but He revealed to us how carnal and fleshly it was for us to do and even showed us in scripture why we shouldn't be drinking at all. He also told us to throw out our hookah, where we occasionally smoked flavored tobacco. He also told me to get rid of my 2 Xboxes, which was probably the most difficult thing for me because I had been a gamer since a young age. I had thousands invested in the hundreds of games I owned. I asked the Lord if I could give it to someone, and He very clearly told me no, that I was to destroy them and throw them away.

He also revealed to us cursed items in our home that we had no idea about. One item in particular was this pretty colorful vase that I bought at an airport gift shop. I was confused as to why He was telling me to throw it away. When I examined it closer, I saw that it was something called a "spirit jar" made by Native Americans to trap spirits. I also had a tree with a bunch of pretty crystals that I used for decoration, which the Holy Spirit told me to throw away. It didn't matter that I had only thought of it as decoration because its intended use was for something evil, and you cannot bless that which is cursed.

Along with all of those items, He began to speak to us about items that were given to us by people we were once in relationships with. He showed us that these items were allowing soul-ties to remain. We spent quite a few weeks going through major house cleaning and repentance.

Not long after He revealed these things to us, He told us to cancel a trip we had planned to the Florida Keys and instead go to a tent revival/deliverance conference for New Year's Eve at Global Vision Bible Church in Mt. Juliet, TN. As we made plans to go there, the attacks from the kingdom of darkness worsened. Jason became very seriously sick. He was running a 105-degree fever and had much trouble breathing for over a week.

At the same time, I had many demonic visitations. Demons would bust into our bedroom door, screaming in my mother's voice and torment me in my dreams all through the night. Then, one night at about 2 am, as I lay on my back in my bed, I felt an animal-like being crawl on top of me. I felt all four limbs, one by one, pull themselves to the top of my bed and then felt its hot breath breathing into my mouth and nose as it was face to face with me. At that moment, I didn't panic because I assumed it was my dog. I opened my eyes to see nothing there in the physical as its breath was still on my face.

The Lord strengthened us and told us to keep going. We began to receive prophetic words about us being torch carriers for revival and having a street evangelism/deliverance/discipleship ministry. It was also prophesied that we were mantled with the bondage breaker anointing and that many would be set free by the working of the Holy Spirit through us.

All of the attacks were meant to keep us from moving forward, gaining freedom, and walking in the truth. We were no longer lulled to sleep by the things of this world. We had stopped walking alongside the devil, and now it had turned into a head-on battle.

Chapter 11

Set the Captives Free

The morning we were to leave for the revival, I awoke with very serious health issues. I had always suffered from stomach issues since I was young, but this day, I woke up with unbearable stomach pain and bloating. I also suddenly started urinating large amounts of blood. I was in so much pain I couldn't even stand. Jason asked if we should even go, to which I replied, "We have no other choice." I knew it was the demons trying to prevent us from going so that they could stay. We packed up the car and headed out, where we had to make a stop almost every hour because of the bladder issues. The Lord had led us to two other destinations prior to the revival.

One place we went, we received a word that the Lord had just now taken us out of Egypt (the world), and now He was to lead us through the wilderness, delivering us from our enemies one by one.

The moment we arrived at the revival, all physical ailments and sickness subsided. We arrived 8 hours early because we heard that many people would be coming and we may not be able to get a seat if we showed up on time. We were glad we were early because the tent was almost full just a few hours later. Around this time, Pastor Greg Locke came to the stage to let everyone know they would be putting on worship music while we waited for the event to begin. He also mentioned that as people begin to worship, we may notice people begin to get set free of demons around the tent. That is exactly what happened. We were still 5 hours from the event even beginning, and hundreds of Christians were being set free of demons and being healed.

By the time the event began, every seat was taken, and any open space on the floor was now occupied by someone standing. They also removed the wall off the backside of the tent so that people who were not able to get in and were standing in the parking lot could still hear the preaching and receive from the Lord. Traffic was also at a standstill for miles down the road. People were parking 5 miles away and walking to the tent in an attempt to get in.

A while into the service, the Lord spoke to me so clearly and said, "I told you to remove your nose ring." See, when we were removing things from our lives that were displeasing to the

Lord, I had thought I heard Him tell me to remove my nose ring, but I kept brushing it off. Well, there was no denying that He was speaking to me about this now because I heard Him so clearly that I was overcome by the fear of the Lord. I didn't quite understand why He wanted me to remove it, and He immediately reminded me of the verses throughout the Bible that refer to the rings in animals' noses. He said to me the purpose of a ring in an animal's nose is to control and lead it and that it was a form of bondage. I removed it as soon as He spoke those words to me.

About five minutes later, there was an altar call for those who believed they needed deliverance. I ran to the front. As hundreds of others ran to the altar with me, one of the altar workers made eye contact with me and went straight in my direction. She laid her hand on the top of my head, and I immediately fell under the power of God. As soon as I went to the ground, these terrifying screams began to come from my mouth. The woman began to cast many demons out of me, including spirits of rage, anger, poverty, and a perverse spirit that was in my eyes from watching pornography in my past. As the spirit of rage left me, I remember the terrifyingly angry screams that came from me, my fists clenched, and I remember feeling like getting up and punching everyone, but it was as if I was pinned to the ground by the power of the Holy Spirit. As these spirits left me, I began to vomit. About 20 minutes later, I was able to get up, and we all celebrated as we brought in the New Year.

The next morning, we returned to the tent as we still had two more conference days. After having received some deliverance, I believed that I was free. But as the morning went on, I began to notice these extremely perverse thoughts that kept coming to my mind that I could not get out no matter how much I tried to think of something else or pray. I began to feel condemned because I didn't know how I could still experience this after deliverance.

After the first message was preached, there was an altar call, and my husband and I both went up. As Pastor Taisha began to pray for everyone corporately, she asked the Lord to send His delivering angels to free His people. At this point, everyone at the altar was on their knees and close together. I began to hear many screams throughout the room and looked up for a moment to see a lady who had been kneeling on the altar steps suddenly do a frog-like backflip as a demon began to scream out of her. Just then, I felt a warmth on the crown of my head, and these screams began to come from me. The Lord was delivering me and hundreds of others throughout the tent without a human hand touching us. I got up from the floor and began to celebrate and thank the Lord for setting me free.

That afternoon, the Lord sent many people from all over the tent to tell us it was time to step into ministry. We received many words confirming things the Lord had already been telling us. A man also walked up to us, pointed at me, and said, "It's time for you to get your passport!" He then told both my husband and me that we needed to start up our ministry and get ordained. We never met this man before, yet he knew only to tell me to get a passport.

As the conference went on, we were just in awe of the miracles we continued to see. God was healing and delivering people all over the tent. We watched as people who couldn't walk began to run, people came off crutches, diseases healed, and so much more. We went and sat in our vehicle for a while and repented to the Lord for not having fully surrendered to Him and allowing Him to work through us in that way. We wept for a while, and then Jason began to ask the Lord to give him even just a finger to pray for.

We went back into the tent for the final service, which happened to be a mass deliverance service. At that point, I had believed I was free, but we went because Jason was believing for deliverance as well. As the worship came to an end, Pastor Taisha Locke began to pray for everyone in the room. I was standing, and my hands were raised as Taisha began to bind specific spirits. As she spoke, I felt my body begin to go limp, and my head fell forward. Then, Pastor Taisha began commanding the spirits that were bound to leave all the people. As soon as she said that, I went flying and took out almost a whole row of chairs; my body was flailing everywhere, so much so that five people were attempting to hold me down, and these screams and voices that were not mine began speaking out of me. As this was happening, I heard hundreds of screams coming from all over the tent. I remember opening my eyes and seeing Pastor Taisha as she began to cast these spirits out of me. The demons hated her and began yelling at her and refusing to leave. While this was all happening, I was fully aware; I just did not have the ability to control much of my bodily movements nor speak from my mouth. When I would try to speak, I would hear my mind's voice saying what I was attempting to speak, but a different voice that was not mine would be saying something different out of my mouth.

After attempting to cast out these demons who were refusing to leave for a while, Pastor Taisha looked at Jason and said, "Are you her husband?" After she found out he was my husband, she said, "You have more authority than me since this is your wife; you cast them out." Many demons began to leave me at this point, and many generational curses were broken. With each curse that was broken, I would vomit or cough up blood. Then, there was a stubborn spirit of witchcraft that refused to leave. It was throwing my body everywhere and laughing just like a witch. One of the five people assisting with my deliverance received a word of knowledge that this spirit came in through witchcraft being done on me by my mother when I was a child. They called my name, and I was able to speak. They told me to renounce the witchcraft done against me and to forgive my mother for doing that. As I spoke, the demon tried to stop me, but I was able to say it. The demon left me immediately after.

My husband and a couple of other people continued to cast the demons out of me, and many left in that hour and a half. As he was casting them out of me, he was also receiving deliverance from demons, and curses were being broken. He wasn't experiencing intense manifestations, but every now and then, he would cough as one would leave and even had a sign of coughing blood and other things up.

I believe there were more than 40 different demons that left me, including spirits of suicide, anxiety, depression, divorce, homosexuality, perversion, religion, and even a spirit of Hinduism that came in through a previous relationship. In that relationship, we had lived together and were fornicating out of wedlock. Though I rejected belief in Hinduism, I allowed him to put up his statues of his "gods" in the house, and we were sleeping together. So this spirit entered through one of those open doors.

As I got up off the floor, I felt as light as a balloon and thought I might just float away. Many people cheered as I stood and was able to praise God. I looked around in amazement, as many people were still being set free all over the tent.

When I got back to the hotel and looked in the mirror, I saw that I had broken blood vessels all over my face due to the intensity of the screams from the demons. I had also almost totally lost my voice, and it took three weeks to get it back.

Chapter 12

Family Revival

As we headed home to Saint Louis, we called quite a few people and shared our testimonies about everything that had happened. While on the phone with our son Dawson, who lives in Louisiana, he and his then-girlfriend were immediately convicted and repented before the Lord. They were pregnant and living together, and they decided to get right with the Lord and get married the next week.

A few weeks later, Dawson was praying in the shower and received the baptism of the Holy Spirit with the evidence of speaking in tongues. Right after Dawson received the baptism of the Holy Spirit, he said there was also a growl that began to come from him, so he immediately called Jason. He asked his dad if he could cast out the demon by phone, and Jason began to pray for him. He described a strong wind that hit him (as he was standing inside his house), and he fell to the floor and began rolling around and coughing up the demon. Just then, his wife walked in the front door and saw what was happening, and she began to pray. As she spoke in English, she suddenly began to speak in tongues as she also received the baptism of the Holy Spirit. They were set on fire for the Lord and began to tell everyone there in Louisiana everything the Lord had done for them.

Meanwhile, back home, Jason began to go through deeper deliverance, and the Lord used me to cast many demons out of him. Then the Lord began to reveal more inside of the both of us, so by the leading of the Holy Spirit, we began to do deliverance on each other many nights. The same power of the Holy Spirit that we saw at the tent revival was now at work in our own lives, especially in our home. After walking each other through deliverance for a while, the Lord told us we would begin helping others get delivered as well.

After only being home from the revival for about three weeks, we received a call from Jason's family that his mother was on her deathbed and all of his siblings would be coming into town from all over the U.S. to say goodbye. So we packed and headed to Louisiana. As we headed that way, Dawson began to tell all of Jason's siblings that we were coming to pray for her and she would get up off of her deathbed. We later learned that many of

Jason's family had gone out drinking the night before and were all mocking us coming to pray for her.

When we arrived at about 2 am, we immediately went into prayer. We slept for a couple of hours and got up again to pray. Jason's mother had been put on a bed in the middle of the living room, and many were crying over her. She had lost all bodily function and couldn't eat or drink. At one point, Jason, his sister Olivia, and I all carried Jason's mom into the bathroom to clean her up. As we sat her on the toilet, I turned my head away while still holding her to give her privacy, and Jason stood on the other side of the wall to give her privacy while Olivia cleaned her up.

Suddenly, I heard Olivia scream, "Jason, there's a demon!" I looked at Jason's mom as the demon began to contort her face; her eyes turned dark, and her lips were turning blue as a demon of death was attempting to take her life. As Jason and a bunch of his brothers ran into the bathroom, Jason began to bind and rebuke the demon. Olivia and a couple of the brothers suddenly began to pray in tongues, which was mind-blowing to me because, as far as I knew, they were not believers. At this point, I was standing in the bathtub because I had tried to get out of the way in all the commotion. After some time, the demon went back down and allowed Jason's mom to breathe. We then brought her back out to the bed in the living room.

At this point, everything had changed. Everyone went from mourning to praying as we all corporately began to go to war for Jason's mom. The atmosphere had completely changed, and the Lord showed up big time. As we continued to try and cast the demon of death out of Jason's mom, suddenly Olivia began to manifest a demon with loud, ear-piercing screams, and her eyes turned black. Three of her brothers had to hold her down as her body was flailing. The same demon that we were calling out of Jason's mom was also in Olivia because it went down the bloodline; Olivia had this one since birth. Because we were calling it out, the demon in Olivia also began to manifest. Jason bound the demon and told it to go back down. When Olivia came to, she said, "Get this thing out of me!" Jason told her he couldn't because she was living in sin (she was living with a woman who she was in a homosexual relationship with and was not surrendered to the Lord), and it would come back with seven more and destroy her. (see Matthew 12:43-45)

A few hours later, Olivia pulled Jason aside and told him that the Lord had been fighting for her, and she was ready to lay her life down and follow Jesus 100%. We asked her if she was sure that she would have to die to herself and not go back; otherwise, these things would destroy her. She assured us that she was ready, so we went back into the house and began to cast many demons out of her. They all manifested and spoke out of her as all her brothers and even some of her young nieces and nephews crowded around her and took authority over the demons. The children saw and believed instantly and began to ask us how they could be saved, so we shared the Gospel with everyone who would listen. Full-on revival began to break out in Jason's childhood home as many believed, worshipped Jesus, received healing and deliverance; prophecy was flowing, and some of Jason's family began washing each other's feet. We hardly slept or even ate as we continued praying for Jason's mom and doing anything else the Lord instructed us to do.

On the third day, the Lord told us it was time to go. We were a bit confused because Jason's mom was still in bed and unresponsive. We obeyed anyway and began to say bye to everyone. A few of them told us we couldn't leave because she wasn't better yet, but we told them they had the same Holy Spirit and were able to believe and do the same as us. Just as we left and stepped foot over the threshold of the front door, we heard a bunch of commotion. We turned around to see Jason's mom get up from bed and take a drink. We praised God, ran back in, gave her a kiss, and left.

Thirty minutes into our drive back to Saint Louis, we received a call from a family in Florida. They stated that the Lord had told them that Jason and I had something to teach them, and they were to humble themselves and ask us to come visit and share with them.

Chapter 13

These Signs Shall Follow Those Who Believe

We made plans to go to Florida, where a couple of Christian families welcomed us into their homes. As we ministered, many of them received deliverance and even healing in a marriage. We were invited back to Florida a couple more times, and people flew from Romania and Austria to visit with us as well. We saw the Lord set people free as there were healings, deliverance, and baptisms of water and the Holy Spirit.

We were ordained in April and began ministering to people locally. Many people would reach out for deliverance, and many times during these appointments, the Holy Spirit would show us that, instead, counsel was needed or even that they needed discipleship prior to walking through deliverance.

Not too long after, we received a call from a Christian family in Chicago who had heard testimonies from families in Florida. They asked if we could come to pray for healing and deliverance. The mother had been diagnosed with cancer, and it was intensifying rapidly as she hadn't eaten anything solid in a month, was constantly vomiting, and was no longer able to walk without assistance. The Lord gave us the go-ahead, and we went to Chicago. After two days of prayer and deliverance, the atmosphere in the home had completely changed. The mother did not have any manifestations as we prayed, but we could sense in the Spirit that big things were happening. That day, the mother sat up and said she was extremely hungry. We went down the street and grabbed some tacos for her, and she scarfed them down. The next day, she was up, taking a shower by herself and cleaning her house. A few weeks after we left, she went back to the doctor, and they ran a blood test to see her cancer cell count. The results came back normal, and they deemed her cancer-free. Praise Jesus!!

Along with traveling from time to time, we were also taking deliverance appointments locally. So we were seeing the Lord set so many free weekly. Miracles became our new normal. The Book of Acts was happening right in front of our very eyes.

At the same time, I entered into what I called my "Job season." I went through major crushing and loneliness. Many people in my life chose to walk away, including friends and family. In this time, I learned to become totally dependent on the Lord. He became my absolute Best Friend. I also suffered through many things in my body; my hair even began to fall out at an unbelievably rapid rate. This brought me deeper into sadness as I cared far too much about my hair. So much so that I began to scramble to try and fix the problem. Nothing worked, so one day, I laid it at the Lord's feet. I repented of vanity and told Him if He didn't want me to have hair, then that's ok; I won't care about it anymore. Shortly after, my hair began to grow back thicker and all the thin and bald spots left.

During this season, we began to suffer financially. We had never been without work, but now we were going months at a time without. However, the Lord always made sure we had everything we needed. We also had many people coming against us, accusing us of doing witchcraft because we were doing deliverance. There were also many who came against us to try and defame our name and business, but we continued trusting in the Lord. He assured me that He had me and that I was going through His refiner's fire.

The closer I got to Jesus, the more He would reveal to me what I needed freedom from. By this time, He was delivering me in the secret place as I would spend time with Him. He revealed to me that there were soul-ties formed and demons that came in through the molestation that happened as a child. As soon as He showed me, I verbally broke the soul ties and told the demons to leave. The Lord gently removed them, and I felt them lift off.

I asked the Lord why it seemed that my deliverance process was taking so long. He told me that many came down through my generations as I was the first Christian in my family. He also showed me that many came through trauma because the devil doesn't play fair and how I had many open doors for most of my life up until that point. Even after I professed Christ and was baptized in the Holy Spirit, I had open doors, and where there are open doors, anything can come in. He also showed me that we have free will and cannot kick out friends, only enemies. Unless we shut those open doors and renounce the legal rights, the demons don't have to leave. Anything that we do that is contrary to God's word is a sin and an open door to the enemy. No, that does not mean every single time you sinned, you got a demon. Just like if you leave your front door open, a bug or spider may or may not come in; it's the same concept. That's why Jesus told us to cast out demons. He never said they would leave when we receive the Holy Spirit, and He never said to pray them away.

He began to speak to me about the Israelites and how He had to take them out of Egypt (the world) completely before He could begin to deliver them from their enemies one by one in the wilderness. He then revealed to me how the Promised Land represents the place where we arrive on our walk where we have dominion over the enemy. That once we arrive there, it will no longer be about us fighting for ground back in our lives, but rather where we have conquered the land and are now keeping the enemy out by guarding the gates and not allowing breaches in our walls.

We have to allow the Holy Spirit to work in our lives. We are saved by GRACE through FAITH. Grace is the working power of the Holy Spirit to stop sin and walk in obedience to the Lord. It is only the working of the Holy Spirit that can totally set you free. We have to listen to what He tells us to do and let grace work in us. He cannot force us to obey Him because we have always had free will, but when we begin to repent and obey, miracles begin to happen. Those secret sins you have always struggled with begin to flee, those thoughts, urges, and impulses? Gone.

It is absolutely possible to live a life where you no longer make a practice of sin, not by your working but by allowing Him to work in you. His word says without holiness, none will see Him. So put your trust completely in Him today. He is a good Father, and every promise of His is true.

Chapter 14

From Glory to Glory

As we continued on, the Lord led us to join the Core Group Mentorship, led by Apostles Stephen and Jenny Weaver, where we experienced major growth. At this point, their ministry had been in revival for a year, and it was very apparent.

The Lord began to speak to us about moving and told us to start selling furniture because He didn't want us to take many things with us. As we started to sell everything, He began to send people to tell us that He has our house picked out for us, and we need only to believe.

As I was still in my "Job season" and every single aspect of my life seemed to be under attack, the Lord continued to assure me that He was bringing me through every bit of it. Though many nights were spent crying myself to sleep, He was right there with me to comfort me. At this point, I had still been dealing with many fears, including the fear of man. It had only been six months since I had been able to pray in front of my husband and other people. But I was still nervous to speak out about many things. I felt trapped in fear, not of demons, but of what others thought about me.

Everything changed once I attended a Core Group Retreat in the Spring of 24'. It was actually a men's retreat, but I went with my husband to fellowship with the other wives who would be there. I had no idea that God was going to radically change everything from the outside of the men's retreat. (the women were not allowed in the services) A woman who became a close friend and her husband began to prophesy over me how the enemy was trying to kill me in my cocoon and that the muzzle the enemy had on my mouth from birth was now coming off. They also prophesied about this very book you are reading, saying that it was about my testimony and how the Lord would set many free through it. I received so much freedom in that moment. Then, that night, Apostle Jenny came out to the hallway where all the wives were hanging out to pray for us. After she laid hands on me, the Fire of the Holy Spirit burned so hot in my belly, and I lay there on the floor weeping so loud that I'm sure people a mile away could hear. It was the deepest cry I had ever had; I knew that deep, deep healing was taking place.

When we returned home, I felt like a brand new person. I felt the boldness of the Holy Spirit inside me like never before. It was as if the Lion of the tribe of Judah was looking out of my eyes, ready to take on anything that came my way.

That week, He instructed me to finish setting up my podcast studio (which I started to build a year ago by His command), and He told me to share my testimony on all social media platforms. This was the first time I was able to talk about every single thing I went through with no pain. It was as if I was talking about someone else.

After I was obedient in sharing my testimony, I experienced even more of a radical acceleration in the Spirit as he began to use me prophetically. My husband and I also began to experience the Glory of the Lord like never before in our home during our times of prayer together. Every day with the Lord is always exciting and an adventure. We look forward to the future and will keep pressing forward in our call in Him, telling the world the Good News and contending for revival.

We continue to see miracle after miracle and will continue going from Glory to Glory.

Among many things, one of the most significant changes I have noticed in myself is my love for others. Before Christ, I used to hate people (especially other women), and after I got saved, I still struggled to be around other people, often labeling myself as an introvert. After He set me free, I have this love for people like no other. I'm not uncomfortable around others and love to walk up to random people and strike up conversations. I suppose that is a great quality to have as an Evangelist. I have also been totally set free from every struggle and sin that I discuss in this book, not by my doing but by His grace. I'm filled with love, joy, and peace that doesn't come from me. If you were to look at my circumstances, you would wonder why I have so much joy and peace.

It's because I stopped asking Him to put out the fires and allowed Him to change me in the fire so that I will come out pure as gold.

He has taken my old identity and completely annihilated it. I am not who I was or the things I did.

So, who am I, you ask?

I am a chosen, transformed, accepted, redeemed, and restored daughter of the Most High God. I was made whole by the Blood of Jesus and will overcome and inherit all things in Christ. I have been crucified with Christ, and it is now no longer I who live but Christ who lives in me. By His grace, I will accomplish the plans He laid out for me to complete and walk out my calling in Christ for His Glory alone, and no demon in hell will stop Jesus' will for my life.

THIS MEANS WAR.

The Lord *is* a man of **war**;
The Lord *is* His name.

Exodus 15:3 NKJV

"Blessed *be* the Lord my Rock,
Who trains my hands for **war**,
And my fingers for **battle**—
My lovingkindness and my fortress,
My high tower and my deliverer,
My shield and *the One* in whom I take refuge..."

Psalm 144: 1-2 NKJV

www.ingramcontent.com/pod-product-compliance
Lightning Source LLC
LaVergne TN
LVHW051813080426
835513LV00017B/1934